ABDO Publishing Company

FISH & GAME

COMMON PHEASANT

D0709932

SAN DIEGO PUBLIC LIBRARY
CHILDREN'S ROOM

3 1336 09438 8452

Sheila Griffin Llanas

visit us at
www.abdopublishing.com

Published by ABDO Publishing Company, PO Box 398166, Minneapolis, MN 55439.
Copyright © 2014 by Abdo Consulting Group, Inc. International copyrights reserved in all
countries. No part of this book may be reproduced in any form without written permission from the
publisher. The Checkerboard Library™ is a trademark and logo of ABDO Publishing Company.

Printed in the United States of America, North Mankato, Minnesota.
112013
012014

♻ PRINTED ON RECYCLED PAPER

Cover Photo: JOHN CANCALOSI / National Geographic Creative
Interior Photos: Al Freng, with special thanks to Autumn Freng & Tucker p. 29; Alamy pp. 12, 20,
    21, 23, 24–25; Getty Images pp. 9, 16; iStockphoto pp. 13, 19, 27; Thinkstock pp. 1, 5, 7, 11,
    15, 19

Editors: Rochelle Baltzer, Megan M. Gunderson, Bridget O'Brien
Art Direction: Neil Klinepier

Library of Congress Cataloging-in-Publication Data

Llanas, Sheila Griffin, 1958- author.
  Common pheasant / Sheila Griffin Llanas.
    pages cm. -- (Fish & game)
  Audience: 8 to 12.
  Includes bibliographical references and index.
  ISBN 978-1-62403-107-6
1. Pheasant shooting--Juvenile literature. 2. Ring-necked pheasant--Juvenile literature. 3.
Hunting--Juvenile literature. I. Title.
  SK325.P5L53 2014
  799.2'46252--dc23
                    2013031871

Contents

Pheasant!

Common pheasants spend much of their lives hidden by grasses, crops, and trees. About 10 million of these ground-dwelling birds live in the grasslands and farmland of South Dakota alone. Yet flocks of pheasants are hard to see!

Finding pheasants is the first step in hunting these wily birds. Footprints in the dirt or snow and the sounds of male roosters crowing are helpful signs. Pheasants can feel vibrations in the ground. So hunters walk quietly to get close to them.

When these game birds are surprised, they burst from hiding. With a flurry of colorful wings, they launch into flight. A bird in the air is the moment hunters wait for.

WILD FACTS!

The ring-necked pheasant is the state bird of South Dakota.

Common, or ring-necked, pheasants are hunted for sport and food. Pheasant meat makes tasty stews and soups. Roasted, the meat is tender and lean.

Good pheasant-hunting states include Iowa, Kansas, Minnesota, Nebraska, and the Dakotas. In Kansas, about 100,000 to 150,000 hunters harvest 400,000 to 800,000 birds each season. Minnesota hunters take an average of 350,000 pheasants. Across the United States, the common pheasant is a top game bird.

Common pheasants are found from southern California to New England and into parts of southwestern Canada. They are even found in Hawaii!

In History

The common pheasant is native to China and East Asia, not North America! Pheasants were first brought to Europe. By the late 1500s, pheasant hunting had grown popular in Britain. Early attempts to bring pheasants to North America failed. These European pheasants were finally successful on the East Coast in the late 1880s.

On the other side of the United States, pheasants first arrived in 1881. American diplomat Owen N. Denny brought them directly from Shanghai, China, to Oregon. After several attempts, pheasant populations began to grow and spread across Oregon and Washington.

In 1892, the Northwest held its first open season. Hunters bagged 50,000 pheasants. In 1906, Massachusetts opened pheasant hunting.

Soon, other states introduced pheasants. They arrived in Kansas in 1906, South Dakota in 1908, Ohio in

1914, and Minnesota in 1916. Over time, the pheasants on either coast spread far enough to mix together. Today, common pheasants remain an important part of the nation's hunting tradition.

For a time, common pheasants were named Denny Pheasants after Owen Denny.

In Balance

In the 1940s, as many as 30 million common pheasants lived in South Dakota. Yet by 1966, the state counted only 2 million. People soon learned that the greatest threat to pheasants is loss of **habitat**.

In the mid-1900s, more houses, towns, and businesses took the place of prairies. Also, farmers used new equipment to cut down overgrown field borders, fencerows, and pastures. They plowed fields in the fall, which left less winter cover for birds. Pheasants could no longer live on those lands.

To support hunting, states began to protect pheasant habitat. They paid farmers to let fields grow wild or follow other land management practices. Also, hunting grounds were stocked with pheasants. Pheasants were hatched and then released in hunting preserves and wild areas.

Some people disagree with stocking. They argue that farm-raised pheasants cannot survive in the wild. Others believe stocking supports hunting. They have seen pen-raised pheasants adapt to living in the wild. Either way, pheasants need a good **habitat** to survive.

Many people want to both hunt and protect common pheasants. To do so, it is helpful to learn all about this popular game bird.

In 2012, Wisconsin had a goal of stocking 54,000 pheasants into 71 hunting grounds. In 2013, Connecticut purchased 15,380 pheasants for state hunting grounds.

COMMON PHEASANT TAXONOMY:

Kingdom: Animalia
Phylum: Chordata
Class: Aves
Order: Galliformes
Family: Phasianidae
Genus: *Phasianus*
Species: *P. colchicus*

Beak to Tail

Common pheasants are in the order Galliformes, with chickens. *Gallus* is Latin for "rooster" and *gallina* means "hen." Male pheasants are called cocks or roosters. Female pheasants are called hens.

Adult male pheasants weigh 2.5 to 3 pounds (1.1 to 1.4 kg). From beak to tail, they measure 33 to 36 inches (84 to 91 cm) long. Their long, pointy tail feathers often take up 20 of those inches! Females have shorter tails. Hens are 20 inches (51 cm) long and weigh only 2 pounds (0.9 kg).

Roosters and hens do not look alike. Roosters have a sharp spur on each leg. Hens don't. A hen's feathers are mainly brown. Roosters shimmer with color! Bright red face **wattles** ring their eyes. Their heads are blue-green or even purple. The white stripe around the male's neck gives common pheasants the nickname "ring-necks." The male's chest is coppery red. Reddish-brown back feathers fade to bluish-green on the lower back.

Each summer, male and female pheasants **molt**. A pheasant's feathers protect it. But, they do not make these birds good fliers! A male's **wingspan** is just 32 inches (81 cm). A female's wingspan is even shorter, at just 24 inches (61 cm) across. This is short compared to the pheasant's body size.

Pheasants take dust baths! They sweep dirt up into their feathers to help clean out old skin and feathers.

To fly, pheasants must flap their wings three times per second. That's fast! For short distances, they can fly up to 60 miles per hour (97 km/h). Pheasants usually fly just a few hundred yards. Rarely, they can stay aloft for up to 2 miles (3.2 km).

WILD FACTS!

A pheasant's tail is horizontal when the bird is feeding. When running, the pheasant holds its tail up at a 45-degree angle.

When cornered, common pheasants may launch into flight. They take off almost straight up! Yet to escape danger, pheasants prefer to run. These birds have long legs designed for running. They stay low and dart left and right to fool their pursuers. To stay safe, pheasants also use their keen senses.

The Common Pheasant

WATTLE

EYE

BEAK

WING

TAIL

LEG

SPUR

FOOT

Common Sense

To understand pheasants, hunters study their senses and behaviors. Pheasants have a poor sense of smell. But, they have good hearing and eyesight. So, hunters must move quietly.

Early morning and early evening are good times to see pheasants. At sunrise, pheasants often go into the open to feed. They peck for food and then move back into hiding.

During the day, common pheasants stay sheltered in thick cover. They **loaf** and **preen**, cleaning and smoothing their feathers with their beaks. Before sunset, they head out to feed again. When night falls, they go to their roosting places to sleep.

In winter, pheasants may eat before sunrise and after sunset. At this time, there is less food available, but they need more energy to keep themselves warm.

To stay cool in hot weather, pheasants shelter in the shade. They also avoid activity during the hottest part of the day. In addition, pheasants act like dogs. They pant! This behavior is called gular fluttering. It releases body heat.

In cold weather, pheasants fluff up their feathers to hold in heat. Body fat also keeps them warm. Still, feathers and fluttering do not protect pheasants from the most extreme weather. For that, they need to live in the right climate.

Under Cover

Pheasants are especially well suited for life in the Midwest plains. Prairies, marshes, and a mix of tree stands and fields make good homes. Pheasants also need clean water. This can come from open water. Or, pheasants can get water from dew and the plants and insects they eat.

Pheasants need the cover of grasses. Tall grasses form roofs over their heads. Cover provides shade from sun and

WILD FACTS!

Common pheasants do not live in mountains, deserts, or extreme wilderness. They do not like dense forests or very dry places.

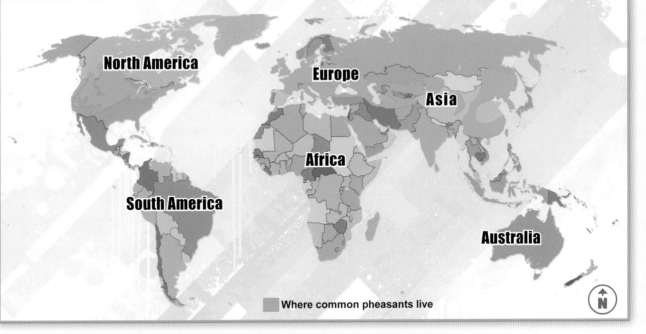

North America

Europe

Asia

Africa

South America

Australia

Where common pheasants live

N

shelter from rain and snow. Under cover, these ground dwellers can hide and run from place to place.

Common pheasants do not **migrate**. They have small home ranges. With enough food and shelter, these may measure just 0.5 to 1 square mile (1.3 to 2.6 sq km).

In spring, birds flock in tall grasses. They just need room to move around at ground level. In winter, they might move to a tree line. Trees shelter them from snow. Those close to fields are perfect. That way, food is near.

Dinnertime

Farmland provides plenty for common pheasants to eat. They eat crops such as corn, barley, soybeans, oats, wheat, sorghum, buckwheat, and sunflowers. After a crop is harvested, pheasants flock to newly mowed fields. They eat waste grains scattered in the dirt.

Rich farm soil provides other foods, too. Healthy weeds grow beside crop fields and in ditches, fencerows, and pastures. Pheasants also eat wild fruits and seeds. These omnivores will even eat insects, small rodents, and snakes. They require a varied diet to stay healthy.

When pheasants swallow food, it goes into a crop. This is a storage cavity. Later when they rest, they **digest** that food slowly. Pheasants do not have teeth. So, they eat gravel. This goes into their gizzards. There, the grit helps grind up their food.

Pheasants have many natural predators. Wild animals such as coyotes, foxes, raccoons, skunks, and owls hunt pheasants for food. Crows, hawks, bobcats, domestic cats, snakes, opossums, dogs, weasels, and minks also go after pheasants and their young.

Pheasants are often seen along gravel roads. This is a good place to eat pebbles and sand to help their digestion.

Having a crop helps pheasants stay safe. They can eat quickly and then head back to safety to digest the food.

Short Lives

Pheasants rarely live more than three years. Luckily, they have high rates of reproduction. Each spring, roosters flap their wings and crow to attract hens. Hens especially like roosters with black on their **wattles**, long tail feathers, and long ear tufts.

After mating, hens make simple ground nests lined with plant material. They lay 7 to 16 eggs, one each

day. The eggs are pale green blue to olive brown. Hens **incubate** them, leaving just briefly for food and water. After 23 to 25 days, all the eggs hatch in one day.

Up to 80 percent of chicks will be lost to disease, predators, and weather.

Each **downy** chick is brown with dark markings on its head and back. It weighs just 0.5 ounces (14 g) and stands three inches (8 cm) tall.

Chicks stay close to their mother. Together, they move to fields with flowering plants. These attract insects, which chicks gorge on to gain weight. At ten weeks old, the **brood** breaks up. Young pheasants go off on their own.

Mating, hatching, and **molting** take energy. So in fall, pheasants relax in cooler weather and fatten up on farm crops. It makes sense then that hunting season opens in fall.

In Season

Hunting rules vary by state. Hunters are responsible for knowing how to legally hunt pheasants wherever they plan to be. They must obtain legal permits and tags and hunt on legal hunting grounds. In states like Wisconsin, a small-game hunting license is required. In others, a special pheasant stamp or permit may also be required.

States set season dates, daily hunting times, and **bag limits**. In many states, pheasant hunting is legal from about October until January. In some areas, hunting closes at 2:00 PM. The daily bag limit is 2 roosters in Wisconsin. In North Dakota, it is 3. The **possession limit** is 12. Again, every state has different regulations.

In most states, it is illegal to hunt hens. Only roosters may be taken. Even harvesting up to 90 percent of males will not harm the next spring's mating season. However, hens need to lay eggs in the spring. That is what keeps the population healthy.

Early in the season, many pheasants are found near farm crops. They **flush** easily. Late-season hunting can be more challenging. Crops have been harvested. Birds move to **dense** grasses. They grow wary of hunters and more alert to danger. They are not as easy to bag!

Together, hunters in North and South Dakota usually bag more than 1.5 million roosters each season!

Safety First

The best and perhaps only weapon for pheasant hunting is a shotgun. Some pheasant experts swear by size-4 steel shot. That size is useful for shooting targets within 50 yards (46 m). Be aware that on many public hunting grounds, lead shot is illegal.

Hunting is no fun unless everyone stays safe. So as with other sports and skills, safety comes first. Good hunters take courses in gun safety training.

For safety, hunters identify their target and what is behind it before shooting.

Firearms must be legal. In the field, hunters must stay alert.

Some states require hunters to stay visible by wearing blaze orange. Hunters always know the location of other hunters in the field. They always identify their target before shooting, and they never shoot toward another hunter.

Gun **safeties** stay on until the hunter is ready to shoot. They only put a finger on the trigger after aiming at a bird. Safety awareness helps prevent hunting accidents.

Bagging a Bird

    Pheasant hunting can be done alone or in groups. Lone hunters can walk quietly into pheasant **habitat** and wait. They watch and listen for signs of the birds. Then, they make noises or sudden movements. And, they walk in a zigzag pattern to **flush** the birds from cover.

    It can be hard to startle a pheasant. With keen senses of sight and hearing, they hear hunters approach. Lucky for hunters, it is possible to corner the birds.

    In groups, hunters can conduct a bird drive. Drivers walk through a field, forcing the birds to run in a certain direction. Posters wait in position for when the birds emerge from cover.

Alone or in groups, many pheasant hunters never leave home without a trusty dog. Hunters rely on trained bird dogs to stand still and point to a bird's location. They also use dogs to **flush** birds from their hiding places.

Some hunters rely on a dog to retrieve pheasants after a successful shot.

The point is to get the bird into the air! Hunters always aim at a bird in flight. They never shoot at the ground. It is unsportsmanlike to shoot a sitting bird. And, this can make birdshot spray dangerously. It may **ricochet** and hit the shooter, a fellow hunter, or a dog.

It takes practice to hit a small, fast, flying target. Hunters aim just ahead of the pheasant. If the bird drops, a hunting dog or a hunter acts quickly to find the pheasant.

Day's End

After a successful pheasant hunt, it is time to prepare the meat for eating. A big reward of pheasant hunting is filling a freezer with food. Pheasant meat can be used in place of chicken in many recipes. It is rewarding to eat and share food from a hunt with family and friends.

Freshly killed pheasants must be handled properly, especially in warm weather. It is good to clean and dress birds immediately after the hunt. This does not take long.

With kitchen shears or a knife and plastic gloves, skilled hunters clean birds quickly. Each hunter has his or her own method. All are careful to avoid cutting the crop or organs that can spread bacteria. The meat must be kept clean, covered, and cool.

In some cases, a wing, the head, or a leg must remain attached to the body. This identifies the bird as a rooster, which means it was legal to hunt.

Pheasant hunting is a favorite pastime for thousands of hunters. It is an American tradition.

At home, hunters clean and safely store their shotguns. Now it is time to share stories of the hunt! Those memories will last forever.

Glossary

bag limit - the number of game animals a hunter is allowed to take in one day.

brood - a group of young birds that were all born at the same time.

dense - closely packed together or crowded.

digest - to break down food into simpler substances the body can absorb. Digestion is the process of digesting.

down - soft, fluffy feathers.

flush - to cause a bird to fly away suddenly.

habitat - a place where a living thing is naturally found.

incubate - to keep eggs warm, often by sitting on them, so they will hatch.

loaf - to spend time relaxing.

migrate - to move from one place to another, often to find food.

molt - to shed skin, hair, or feathers and replace with new growth.

possession limit - the number of daily limits, or total number of game animals, a hunter is allowed to keep in the field or in transit.

preen - to use the beak to groom feathers.

ricochet (RIH-kuh-shay) - to bounce or skip off a surface.

safeties - devices used to prevent a weapon from firing by accident.

wattle - loose skin usually hanging from the head or neck of a bird.

wingspan - the distance from one wing tip to the other when the wings are spread.

To learn more about common pheasants, visit ABDO Publishing Company online. Web sites about common pheasants are listed on our Book Links page. These links are routinely monitored and updated to provide the most current information available.
www.abdopublishing.com

Index